THE BEST OF
C. Barsotti

THE BEST OF

C. Barsotti

RAVETTE BOOKS

First published by Ravette Books Limited, 1989

Many of the cartoons in this book were
reprinted from *The New Yorker, USA Today,
Punch, Texas Monthly, The New York Times and
The Kansas City Star and Times*.

Printed and bound in Great Britain
for Ravette Books Limited,
3 Glenside Estate, Star Road, Partridge Green,
Horsham, Sussex RH13 8RA
by Ebenezer Baylis, Worcester

ISBN 1 85304 181 5

"For Ramoth, once again and forever"

"Yes, I'm free to talk, dear. Yes, liver and onions would be fine."

"I'm sorry. Mr. Mitchell is only painted on the wall."

4:55 P.M.

"What's this, Jenkins? Are you absent today or something?"

"Then, gentlemen, it is the consensus of this meeting that we say nothing, do nothing, and hope it all blows over before our next meeting."

"They'll teach you tricks. _I'll_ teach you tricks of the trade."

"That's not going to work in <u>this</u> office, buddyboy. The Boss and I are both cat people."

"Gee, I hope I never want a treat _that_ badly."

"*Look, if bad people come, and I don't think any bad people <u>will</u> come, you won't be expected to scare them off by yourself.*"

"I've been hoping I'd be trained as an attack dog, but so far it's just been sit, stay, and fetch."

"Yes, most strangers *are* nice, but we bark at them all, anyway."

"*Learn a trade. You won't be cute forever.*"

"It is we."

"Yes, we are considered man's best friend, but no, we are not allowed on the couch."

"Nobody's the cutest, you're _all_ cute."

"O.K., O.K., I'll run back to the store and get the kind you like."

*"But it's the nicest kennel in the county and we've been planning
this trip for a year and it is only for two weeks."*

"Oh! Your husband really _is_ a clown."

"I'm afraid you'll have to be a little more specific, Ma'am."

"*Wornal, take this plant out and kill it.*"

WHILE YOU WERE AWAY

"I answer the phone 'Dickerson here' because I'm Dickerson and I'm here. Now what the hell do you want, Martha?"

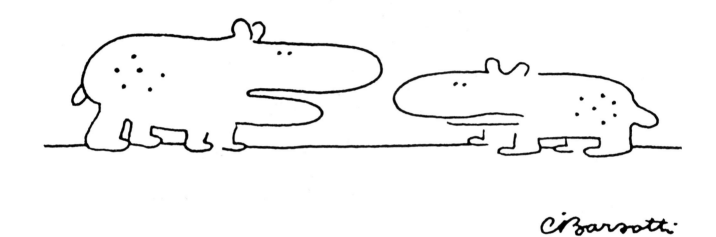

"I know it sounds exciting, but you're not a wildebeest,
and that's that."

*"I'd like to place a person-to-person call, operator, to —
oh, just anybody."*

"He can't come to the phone now. He's indulging the licence society affords those it deems creative."

DETERMINING WHO'S BOSS

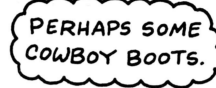

*UNCLE ED WENT OUT WEST AND BECAME A
COWBOY*

"It was three years ago today that Clovis went out West for the big chilli cook-off and was never heard from again."

"I just want you to know, Elwood, if I'd been looking for a good guy tonight I'd have gone to a Roy Rogers movie."

"Oh, stop acting like a junior partner."

I GRANT YOUR WISH. HENCEFORTH YOU WILL BE KNOWN AS FANG.
CBarsotti

"That's what I'm here for, pal, now what do you want fetched?"

"It's agreed then, we'll name him Rex and keep him."

"They feed me, I fetch. It's a wonderful example of a symbiotic relationship."

"*Well, it's not as if you didn't give her some cause to yell at you.*"

LONG LUNCH

"No, sorry, I haven't seen your ball."

"I hope I never lose my sense of wonder."

"Hey, do you want to hear a good cat joke?"

"Yes, sergeant, I'm sure, footsteps in the kitchen. Now ask your
men to hurry please."

"Charles, I've had it with you and your goddam moods."

LATE FOR WORK

"Not now, I have desperadoes to catch."

"You want to <u>see</u> the treat before you roll over? O.K., I can understand that."

"Pookie? I _love_ it. Well, it's nice to meet you, _Pookie_."

"My bark is worse than my bite, but my bark isn't all <u>that</u> terrifying either."

"It's oat-bran flakes with skim milk; you don't <u>need</u> it and you don't <u>want</u> it."

"I wish they'd get me a flea collar."

"Ace carpet cleaners? Could you come <u>right</u> over?"

"Would you like to hear some music while you hold?"

"Oh, hi, dear. I was just thinking of you."

"He's in the counting house. That's Extension 5198."

"The chimney's a fake."

HARDENED CRIMINAL

"Wimp."

"You think you're cute don't you?"

COWBOYS NEWS

"I'm a good guy, ma'm, as you can tell by my pleasant countenance."

SAGEBRUSH REBELLION

"Here's a song I wrote about fifteen minutes ago when my little gal
left me for a bi-sexual backstage caterer."

"Now I ain't no spangled, rhinestone cowboy, I'm the real thing."

"*Now this nickname, Wild Bill, where in the hell
did you get that?*"

"*Castle.*"

"*Edward the Good? Well, Eddie, we'll be the judge of that.*"

THE PHANTOM OF THE GARDEN

TOUGH GUYS

"So you're little Bobbie; well, Rex here has been going on and on about you for the last 50 years."

"Yes, grand, wonderful, and indeed, at times, noble, but you must always keep in mind they are only human."

"*Are you Prince?*"

"*Aw, come on, I didn't mean anything. Gosh, I'm Irish, Italian, French and English, so I'm a mutt too.*"

"I accept this on behalf of mutts everywhere."

REGULARS

"*Of course. Your reputation precedes you, sir.*"

"First, Birchfield, let me say that it does these old eyes good to see real passion in the work place once again."

"Prosperity doth bewitch men, seeming clear;
But seas do laugh, show white, when rocks are near."

"Just say what you have to say, Harwell, and get out."

"Your motto is 'Dare to reach for greatness'? Goodness, I don't _have_ a motto."

"We're offering you the job on probation, Whitlock. You have
three months to become one of us."

"There! There she is! Now go back to the agency and write something for her!"

"Oh, Edgar, I love it when you justify greed in such glowing moral terms."

NO
MESSAGES

C Barsotti

"*Laugh, and the world laughs with you, but not in the Accounting Department.*"

"Oh, boy, liver chunks. No, I won't be late tonight, dear."

"Very well, I'll unbend a little."

"Now, now, 'It's a dog-eat-dog world' is only an expression, a very unfortunate expression."

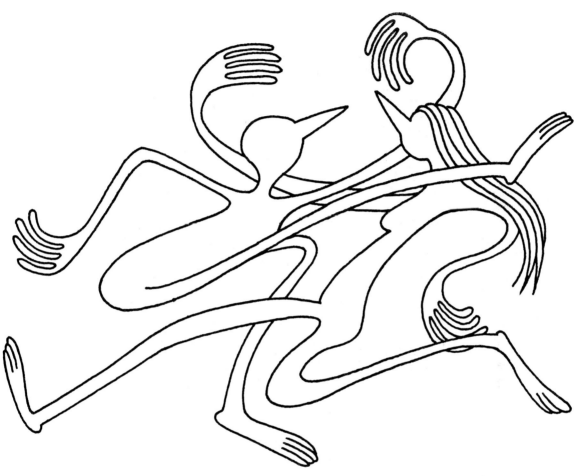

WHAT KINGS TALK ABOUT LATE AT NIGHT

"Off hand I'd say your offer sounds very attractive, but I'm afraid
you'll have to call me back when my wise men are here."

"*If he likes me better, sire, I'm sure it's only because I feed him.*"

"Oh, _yeah_, we hang around together all the time."

"Dog bites man, eh? Great, we'll hold the front page."

"Well, if just once they'd say, 'Hey, Bowser, we're thinking of going out tonight, would you hang around and guard the place?', maybe I _would_ hang around and guard the place."

"*There.* Now knock it off."

"I'll pencil you in for Sunday."

"*Monsieur, may I suggest. . .*"

"*Where is it written that we accountants can't express <u>our</u> individuality?*"

"Do you have to do that now?"

"*I'm learning to let go and have fun.*"

"Well, if you'll stay out of Mrs. Robbins' garden, I'm sure she'll stop saying those things about you."

"Whoops, nearly made a big mistake, this wine is much too good
to sell to a common mongrel."

"Have you no shame?"

"Look, they throw it, you bring it back. Don't rock the boat."

"That's not Smith. Smith's not that tall."

"See, there, Perkins, I told you if you switched from three-martini lunches to a high-carbohydrate diet you'd feel perkier in the afternoons."

"*Ogden, you're taking yourself too damn seriously.*"

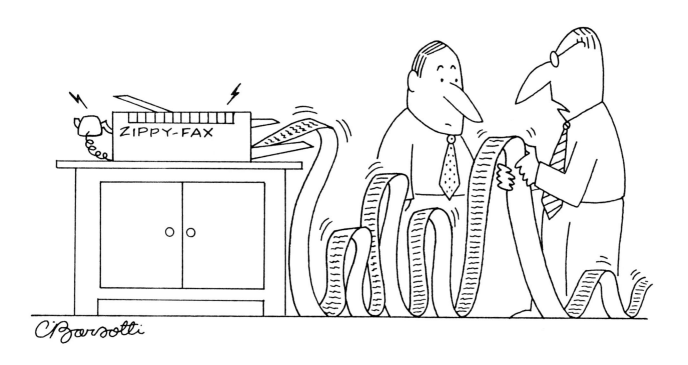

"*Is he angry? Oh, yeah, this time he's <u>really</u> steamed.*"

"*Somebody come play with this damn dog!*"

"You're right, he is smiling. Now get him to stop."

"Oh, I _would_ bite, but only if the cause were just."

"I'm back. Move."

"There, I did it. I called Buckingham Palace, but they said, no,
you couldn't come and play with the corgis
because you're just a mutt."

*"As unbelievable as it may seem to you today, this court was once
a puppy, too."*

"I can get another sofa pillow, that's not what hurts. What hurts is my loss of faith in you."

"But, dear, if <u>I</u> didn't chew up this sofa pillow and <u>you</u> didn't chew up this sofa pillow, what on earth do you suppose happened to this sofa pillow?"

"What the hell is this stuff?"

"O.K., O.K., you're <u>not</u> sacked."

"Well, if you heard a whistle, why didn't I hear a whistle?"

"Oh, I think after a few days in the country I'll be O.K."

"R-e-x, Rex. If you can master perspective, you can learn to sign these things without my help."

"And were you good while I was out?"

IN PURSUIT OF EXCELLENCE

"Today, gentlemen, we must justify our existence."

"No, Hoskins, you're not going to do it just because I'm telling you to do it. You're going to do it because you believe in it."

"Go! Go! Go! Go!"

"I'm sorry, Edgar, but now that I've taken you apart and put you
back together you no longer interest me."

"Keep talking, I'm listening."

"There are cat people and there are dog people and there are people who are a little of both and people who are neither. Each type of person can be nice in his own way, but generally speaking you'll be better off sticking with dog people."

"Oh, grow up."

"As is our custom, we will begin the meeting with the pledge of allegiance to the pack."

"They're out. It's the damn answering machine."

"Yeah? Well, I happen to know that <u>you're</u> not supposed to be in here, either."

"O.K., laugh, but this is going to be my ticket out of here."

Dear Trixie,
 Having a wonderful time. Miss you and wish you were here.

LONE WOLF

"You're history, Leonard."

DRESS FOR SUCCESS

"The old man calls these meetings on an hour's notice and says come prepared. How prepared can you get in an hour?"

"Someday, my son, that will mean you."

"Hello, Sainsbury's? Do you sell dog food for very naughty puppies? No? Well, I certainly don't blame you. Thank you, Sainsbury's, and goodbye."

"What the hell did you do with your day before I retired?"

"It's O.K. I'm not really in the mood, either."

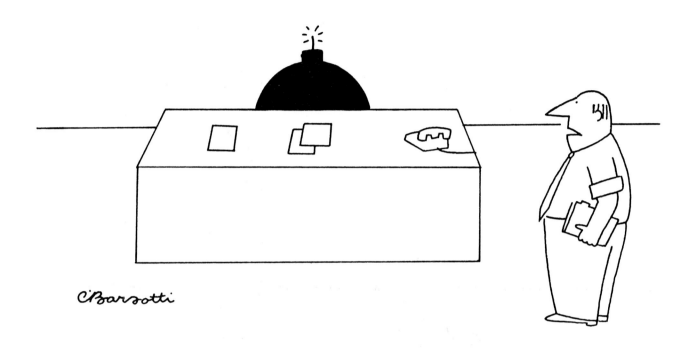

"Nevermind, I'll come back later."

"From here it looks like liver and onions."